Anointings and Mantles

Anointings and Mantles

Ed Dufresne

Ed Dufresne Ministries
Temecula, California

Unless otherwise indicated, all scriptural quotations are from the *King James Version* of the Bible.

Anointings and Mantles
ISBN 0-940763-09-5
Copyright © 1994 by
Ed Dufresne Ministries
P.O. Box 186
Temecula, CA 92593

Published by
Ed Dufresne Ministries
P.O. Box 186
Temecula, CA 92593

Editorial Consultant: Phyllis Mackall

Contents

Chapter 1

Concerning Spiritual Gifts

Paul writes in First Corinthians 12:1, "Now concerning *spiritual gifts*, brethren, I would not have you ignorant."

Later in this chapter, Paul adds that he does not want us to be "stupid, misinformed, or ignorant" concerning the *gift ministries* God has set in the Church.

I'm convinced that before you begin to teach or study the spiritual gifts outlined in First Corinthians 12, you need to go back to the eleventh chapter, where Paul lays the groundwork by teaching about *discerning the Lord's Body*.

Actually, that's what you're doing when you study these two chapters: You're discerning *the gifts of the Spirit* in the Body of Christ as well as *the gift ministries* that God set in the Church. Praise God for every type of ministry!

Prophets, as you probably know, are different. Sometimes they will "camp" on one subject until the situation changes. At other times, they will zero in on different things.

Often when preaching I say to myself, "How did I get off on *that* subject?" Then I'll receive a letter that says, "I had a problem, and you hit the nail right on the head!"

That's my job. As a prophet, I'm a "stump puller." Of course, stump pullers don't get much credit for anything; they just clear everything out of the "field." Later the other gift ministries — apostle, evangelist, pastor, teacher — come along and till the ground, nurturing the tender plants in God's garden.

In the twelfth chapter of First Corinthians, Paul also refers to you, the everyday Christian. Every one of you is set in the Church, the Body of Christ, and every one of you needs to discern your part in the Body.

Paul said in First Corinthians 12:28, "God hath set some in the church, first *apostles*, secondarily *prophets*, thirdly *teachers*, after that *miracles*, then *gifts of healings, helps, governments, diversities of tongues.*"

God has set them in the Church! We need to *discern* each part God has set in the Church. We don't need to *criticize* each other.

For example, a man who flows in the gifts of the Spirit, but does not have a strong preaching or teaching gift, needs to work on developing that gift and needs to be under a pastor or a teacher to help keep his ministry straight, so he'll stay in line with the Word of God.

We Need Each Other

We need each other. Because we supply each other's spiritual needs, we shouldn't criticize how another Christian functions. God has set that person in the Church for a purpose.

Those who don't operate strongly in miracles need to be careful not to make fun of those who do have miracle anointings, and those who flow in miracle anointings need to realize the necessity for those who teach and bring balance and stability with the power of the Word and the Spirit.

If we concentrate on just one type of ministry without discerning the *whole* Body of Christ, we will miss out on something vital to our life, because we need every other part in the Body to remain healthy spiritually and even physically.

Those who do not discern the Body properly will become weak and sickly, and will die physically prematurely.

People are blessed when a variety of anointings are exercised in meetings.

Prophecy

There are those whom God has not set. They have set themselves and said, "I am an apostle, and I am a prophet, and I am this, and I am that."

Shortly you will see some of them drop dead, even in the pulpit, because they are lying to the Holy Spirit. And because the Head of the Church never set them into the Church to walk in that office.

You'll hear it said, "My, my, you know that preacher just keeled over in the pulpit. He must have been burned out."

No, saith the Lord, you shall see some of those go off the scene who get up and absolutely lie, saying, "I am this and I am that," but I never told them that they were in those offices.

But there will be those who will walk in the mighty power of God. I have set these in their offices. They are not ignorant of the things that pertain to the Spirit, and they will walk in the office that I have set them in.

And they will rise up in these last days, and they will walk in the anointing, the gifts, and the equipment of their offices. Oh, how the Body of Christ will be blessed, because they will be coming on the scene.

Yes, the fivefold ministries and those that I have set in the Church will even come into cities. The pastor will work together with them as a team, and blessings will be conferred because of their unity, saith the Lord of hosts.

God set every part or member in the Body of Christ. We need them all! If you do not discern the local church, you will be weak spiritually. Yes, you might fool people as you operate in the gifts and so forth, but you will always be weak spiritually, *because God has set the local church in the Body of Christ.*

Manifestations of the Holy Spirit

Let's continue in First Corinthians 12. The fourth verse

3

says, "Now there are [differences and] diversities of gifts, but the same Spirit."

Although Paul is referring here to *the gifts of the Spirit,* I believe he is also pointing to *the gift ministries,* because they're mentioned in this same chapter.

Verse 5: "And there are differences of administrations, but the same Lord." The word "administration" means "services, ministries, and offices." Notice the Lord is the Head of the administrative arm of this big "corporation," the Body of Christ.

Verse 6: "And there are diversities of operations, but it is the same God which worketh all in all." God is the One who operates it to accomplish things done in the Body of Christ.

Verse 7: "But the manifestation of the Spirit is given to every man to profit withal." I don't want to sound spooky, but "manifestation" means "appearing." There are different ways the Holy Spirit manifests, or appears, and we are not to make fun of them!

Mocking a Manifestation

I was guilty of this years ago, watching a fellow on television. He'd stick his fingers in someone's ears and say, "Now, deaf spirits, come out!" And he'd put his finger on their mouth and command the dumb spirit to come out. Then he'd say, "Say baby. Ba-by. Ba-by."

And I was sitting there laughing and saying, "Ba-by," mocking this man of God. It seemed funny then, but I was mocking the way the Spirit of God was operating through him.

And God said, "I want to ask you a question."

(When He wants to ask you a question, you're in trouble! You've had it!)

I said, "What is it?"

He said, "How many auditoriums do *you* fill up?"

"Well, I go down here on the Indian reservation, and about 16 people show up." I knew He had me.

Don't criticize because of the way different manifestations of the Holy Spirit flow through different people.

Don't Leave Out the Spirit

If we're not careful, we can get into one mindset. Then we will say things like, "Bless God, I'm a Word man. Unless it's in the Word..." Well, it *is* in the Word. It's in the verses we've been studying.

You can be such a stickler for the Word that you leave out the Spirit! *We need both the Word and the Spirit.*

In 1971, when the anointing came into my right hand and manifested itself by heat and a burning sensation, I didn't know what it was. I didn't know anyone else operating with that manifestation, and people were making fun of me because of it.

In one of my meetings, I described how the tangible healing anointing felt like a hot silver dollar being held in my hand. Then one man got up and said, "*I* haven't got silver dollars in *my* hand that are real hot." He was criticizing me. He was jealous because he didn't operate under that kind of anointing.

I never asked for that kind of anointing in the first place, but I knew what God had spoken to me, so I continued operating in it.

Chapter 2

Anointings Within and Upon

There's a verse in Isaiah that says that the anointing destroys the yoke (Isaiah 10:27). *The anointing* completely devastates it, and it disappears!

You also know the verse in First John which refers to *the anointing within* (1 John 2:20). I call it "the personal anointing" — the personal anointing for my everyday life, to lead and guide me into the things of the Lord.

This personal anointing even leads me into what kind of car to buy. If you had listened to the Holy Spirit, you never would have bought that lemon of yours! You see, the Holy Spirit, the Comforter, will lead, guide, and teach us, as Jesus promised. We need to listen to Him. We need to develop our personal anointing.

Whenever people receive Jesus as the Lord of their life, the Holy Spirit bears witness with their spirit that they are a child of God, so they are born of the Spirit. They have an anointing within, whether or not they ever receive the baptism of the Holy Spirit with the evidence of speaking in tongues.

Another important type of anointing is *the anointing that comes upon us.* Jesus talked about this anointing, which is for service, or to help other people. He said of Himself, "The Spirit of the Lord is *upon* me...." So this isn't our personal anointing.

In Luke 4:18,19, Jesus said, "The Spirit of the Lord is upon me, because he hath anointed me to preach the gospel to the poor; he hath sent me to heal the brokenhearted, to preach deliverance to the captives, and recovering of sight to the blind, to set at liberty them that are bruised, to preach the acceptable year of the Lord."

Actually this is the call, corporately speaking, to the whole Church — to preach the Gospel!

Differences in the Two Anointings

Now I want to touch upon some things I think we've often missed. For many years I have backed off from saying certain things for the simple fact that you can't build a ministry on the supernatural. I hope you know that: You can't build a ministry on the supernatural or on the ministry gifts. *You must build a ministry on the Word of God.*

The anointing *upon* comes and goes, enabling you to stand in different offices. But the anointing *within* comes and abides with you. It's there not only to teach and guide you in the things of the Lord, but also to build character in you.

The reason why many people don't have any character is because they're not listening to the Holy Spirit.

The Holy Spirit will lead and guide you into all truth. Although you should develop this anointing more than any other, you must not "throw the baby out with the bath water." We need all of these anointings.

Anointings Within the Mantle

"The Spirit of the Lord is upon me...." We know that Jesus made this statement many times. The anointing came upon Him, covering Him like a coat. I like to say that *a mantle* came upon Him. (I like to use the word "mantle".)

There are many different types of *anointings* in a *mantle*. For example, there are different types of anointings in the mantle, or office, of a pastor.

I have been around a pastor who truly was a pastor, yet he

couldn't preach his way out of a wet paper sack. He wasn't even a good teacher. But, boy, could he pastor! He loved and empathized with his people, and the people loved him.

Even though a teaching center was just down the street and his flock would go there for special meetings, they'd come home to be around that pastor. Why? *Because he had a mantle.*

He was a shepherd. Even though he couldn't preach that well, he was still a "feeder." A shepherd is a feeder; he feeds the sheep.

Don't Judge Other Ministries

That's why you shouldn't go around judging different ministries, saying, "He's kind of dry." The next time you have a death in your family, call the television evangelist you give all your tithes to. When you get sick, go to *his* door.

You aren't going to find him, because that isn't his call or equipment. You need a shepherd at such a time. You must realize we need all these varieties of anointings.

We need all of these varieties of anointings — even those teachers you think are "dry" because they don't shout and spit.

Jesus preached, "The Spirit of the Lord is upon me...." Notice He didn't preach about titles. A lot of people are going by titles now. Everyone has a title. "What are you?" is the first question some people ask.

In some churches, they make all the people call certain members by these titles: Apostle So-and-so, Prophet So-and-so. After watching them for a while, I can tell if they're really in that office or not.

You may have a title, but you're known by your anointing. You're known by the mantle you have and what you walk in. You need to walk in your mantle and your authority, because if you don't believe in it, no one else will believe in it.

In fact, if you are a pastor, unscrupulous people will come

and try to take your church away from you.

Yielding to Familiar Spirits

A person I know went to a prophet's meeting. Those in charge announced, "After the service, we're going to go into a back room and this prophet will give everyone a word."

Things like this bother me for the simple fact that I can't turn the prophetic gift on and off like that, and they can't either. If the anointing doesn't come and you operate anyway, you're yielding to something else. Don't forget, familiar spirits know where you live and everything else about you!

My acquaintance went into the back room afterwards, and the so-called prophet prophesied over him, "You're going to be a great, great, great — not just two "greats" but three — apostle to the nations."

I heard the tape. First of all, no one but the Lord Jesus Christ is great, but this "prophecy" was very appealing to the flesh. Second, I couldn't even get this person to attend church regularly, so how is he going to be an apostle to the nations? I advised him to put the "prophecy" on the shelf, where it belongs.

Chapter 3

Coming Through the Cross

W hen many people teach on the prophet's ministry, they focus on his role in the Old Testament. No, *you've got to bring the prophet's ministry through the cross of Calvary.* Then you can examine it in a new light. So always bring your teaching out of the Old Testament through Calvary. It will keep your doctrine straight.

In the Old Testament, they danced with all their might. Not God's might; *their* might. Today we, too, are trying to do a lot of things without the anointing. We think we can do just about anything without it. Well, we can't do anything without it. We can only do what Jesus says to do.

We're discussing different anointings that God sets on different ministries. My goal is to help get people back on the right track. I've gotten off before, and if you would be honest and not lie to the Holy Spirit, every one of you would admit that you have gotten off, too. We all have, because we're human.That's why it's good for young ministers who have the gifts in operation to be around seasoned ministers with their type of anointing; they can develop and mature their spiritual gifts and callings.

Acts 10:38 says, "How God anointed [or covered over] Jesus of Nazareth with the Holy Ghost and with power: who went about doing bad things to people to teach them things." No, that isn't what it says! God anointed Jesus to do what? To help people! That's the reason you get anointed: to help people, to set people free.

Your Anointing Is for Others

The anointing that comes upon is not for you personally; you are supposed to use it to help others. In fact, it is extremely difficult for most ministers to appropriate the healing anointing for themselves. I knew preachers who have had great healing ministries, yet they became sick and died with sickness and disease. Why? *Because they didn't appropriate healing for themselves!* Preachers have to live off the anointing within just as all other believers have to.

There have been times when I've been attacked with sickness when I was on the road. I've laid my right hand on myself, trying to get that anointing to work for me, but it didn't. I must "turn the switch of faith on" for myself, just like you do.

Titles seem so important to the natural, fleshly world, but I never need to ask preachers what type of ministry they have. When I watch them minister for a while, I can see which anointing comes on them.

The anointing came on Jesus. He went everywhere and preached to the people. *He brought attention to the healing anointing that was on His life.*

A New Look at an Old Story

Now let's look at the story in Mark 5 of the woman with the issue of blood.

> **And a certain woman, which had an issue of blood twelve years,**
>
> **And had suffered many things of many physicians, and had spent all that she had, and was nothing bettered, but rather grew worse,**
>
> **When she had heard of Jesus, came in the press behind, and touched his garment.**
>
> **For she said, If I may touch but his clothes, I shall be whole.**
>
> **Mark 5:25-28**

In other words, her medical insurance ran out! Sometimes this happens to us. We spend everything we have, and *then* we run to God with our problem.

Another translation renders the woman's statement as, "If I may touch His *mantle*, I may be whole." Her remark makes the story much clearer to me, because I want to look at her story the way she looked at it.

The Old Testament Prophet's Ministry

In those days, before the cross, the Jews went to their prophets to receive guidance, healing, and everything else of a spiritual nature.

Why? Because *there was a tangible anointing in the mantle of the prophet;* and in most prophets today, under the New Testament, it's the same way. However, you no longer need to go to a prophet for guidance or healing.

In fact, you must be very careful of extreme teachings about prophets. If you're not careful, these teachings end up in heavy submission-type doctrines where you've got to go to the prophet to find out everything! You don't need to do this; you've got the Holy Spirit within to guide you.

If I were to come to your church and you advertised that a prophet was coming to town who would tell you about your future, the church would be packed out. That's the way the world is.

If a true prophet gives you a word, he won't lay out your entire future, because that way you wouldn't walk by faith.

The world is turning to divination. Millions of people are calling late-night 900 numbers where psychics advise them about their future, their personal life, their finances, and so forth. Why do they do this? *Because the world doesn't want to walk by faith.* They want everything laid out for them.

A Woman Who Walked by Faith

The woman with the issue of blood is a good example of a person who walked by faith.

> **For she said, If I may touch but his clothes [mantle], I shall be whole.**
>
> **And straightway the fountain of her blood was dried up; and she felt in her body that she was healed of that plague.**
>
> **And Jesus, immediately knowing in himself that virtue [power] had gone out of him, turned him about in the press, and said, Who touched my clothes [mantle]?**
>
> Mark 5:28-30

Someone made a demand on Jesus. *Someone pulled on His anointing.*

> **And his disciples said unto him, Thou seest the multitude thronging thee, and sayest thou, Who touched me?**
>
> **And he looked round about to see her that had done this thing.**
>
> **But the woman fearing and trembling, knowing what was done in her, came and fell down before him, and told him all the truth.**
>
> **And he said unto her, Daughter, the fact that I am a prophet of God is what made thee whole.**
>
> Mark 5:31-34

Is that what Jesus said to her? Do you know your Bible? What does it say? Jesus told her, "Daughter, *thy faith hath made thee whole...."* Her faith had made a demand on that anointing. She even said it: "If I may touch...if I may do it."

By Faith the Woman Prophesied Her Healing

She was prophesying her healing when she said it. She made a demand on Jesus' anointing.

You don't come to see man, because he can't heal you.

14

However, the anointing that is in his mantle can heal you, and you can make a demand on that mantle of anointing.

If I make a demand on the mantle that falls on a man, it doesn't bring attention to the man; it brings attention to God, because He is the Operator of those anointings He has set in the Church. That's why I don't think it's wrong to bring attention to the anointing — just don't bring attention to yourself!

Many familiar spirits are roaming around today. *Usually, if a familiar spirit is operating in a man, it will always bring attention to the man instead of giving all the glory to God.*

The Corporate Anointing

Corporately speaking, there is an anointing on the whole Church. In the Great Commission, Jesus instructed the Church, "Lay hands on the sick, and they shall recover" (Mark 16:18).

God anoints some people to heal, just like He anoints some to preach and do other things, because there are different types of anointings. When the Body of Christ starts to discern these things, great blessings will come, corporately speaking.

We also need the prophet's ministry. The prophet's ministry has actually been suppressed. I myself have backed off from expressing it fully for various reasons, but no more. The Lord started dealing strongly with me about walking fully in the prophet's ministry, and I listened.

Stirring Up the Flesh

Remember, you're not the one who sets people in the Church; God does. There are many cases today of "people setting people," like that group that was trying to set up that person I knew as an apostle. Even though he loves God, he's no apostle. It's a struggle to get him to church.

Do you know what an apostle really is? First, he demonstrates all the fruit of the Spirit as well as outstanding gifts of the Spirit in his life. I personally believe that an apostle has the ability to operate in *all* the fivefold offices. God gives him that ability *as the need arises*. This ability is included in the anointings in his mantle.

I like to observe and learn, and I've noticed something that happens around some of the younger prophets. A lot of them prophesy all the time; when they're sitting around lunch tables, and every place else. They just turn it on.

They excuse their behavior by saying, "Well, we're told to stir up the gift!" But this admonition by Paul in Second Timothy 1:6 refers to the fire of God in you — not to the prophet's anointing — because the gifts operate *as the Spirit wills* (1 Corinthians 12:11).

You can't stir up the gift of prophecy; God has to stir it up.

Usually people who prophesy all the time, prophesy the same things when they're out of the pulpit that they prophesy when they're in the pulpit, with one important difference: *The anointing is not on them when they're out of the pulpit.* They're prophesying in the flesh!

There are times, as the Spirit wills, when God will use me in the prophet's ministry, and I can prophesy over everyone in a group. But it's as the Spirit wills, not as I will.

On the other hand, because of the misuse of the gift, we are tempted to completely back off from the things of God. I've been concerned about this. Yes, we need to be careful of error, yet we don't need to get in fear and completely back off, either.

How the Anointing Comes

The anointing is God's business as Operator and Director of the Church. This is the way it operates: God says, "Now, the people are coming to this meeting tonight, and I'm going to orchestrate it. This is what I want done." He tells Jesus, the Administrator, and Jesus instructs the Holy Spirit, the One who manifests God's will.

We ministers must be sensitive enough to follow the Spirit of God, allowing Him to appear and manifest through us. That's why we need to be found before the Lord and not socializing too much with the people. That's why we're not given to "serve tables" (Acts 6:2). That's why God has sent us the ministry of helps. We've got to be before the Lord in prayer and meditation so we can walk in that anointing.

The Bible speaks of waiting on the Lord, or waiting on your ministry (Romans 12:7). One translation even talks about *"practicing* before the Lord."

Often when I'm waiting on the Lord, I get things in the Spirit. God will start showing me things. He might say, "Now when you go over there tonight, you will see a woman in a red dress. She's got this problem, and I want you to do thus and so..." We must follow through on what we see.

There's something blessed about waiting on your ministry — waiting for the anointing to come. Sometimes I hold meetings where I minister to ministers, and I just love it. I believe God has called me to minister to ministers.

With Signs Following

"And God wrought special miracles by the hands of Paul" (Acts 19:11). *Special miracles* are extraordinary miracles — unusual demonstrations of power, miracles of an unusual nature.

Although God is going to raise up people who will have miracles of an unusual nature, I am not a miracle-chaser. Miracles follow me when I preach the Word of God. Actually, they follow the Word (Mark 16:20). If you're full of the Word, miracles will follow you, too.

It's interesting to me that many churches claim that they preach the Word of God, yet they never have any miracles! You've got to be careful that you don't preach your little pet doctrines instead of the uncompromised Word of God.

The woman with the issue of blood said, "If I may touch but His mantle. If I may make a demand on that anointing of His..."

Do It God's Way

Sometimes we ministers need to check our lives and go back to the thing God told us to do. Remember when God spoke to you? Did you get away from what He told you to do? It's very important that you do it the way God wants it.

God instructed one man to spit on people. Tremendous miracles occurred in his ministry when he did this in his prayer lines. If other ministers tried to imitate him in the flesh, they would get in trouble, or get "slapped."

What would have happened if he got criticized and never did it anymore? The Church wouldn't have profited from his special anointing.

There are many things we ministers have backed off from, and as a result, the Church isn't profiting from them. I myself have backed off from doing certain things I knew I should do in the Spirit.

How to Overcome Discouragement

If you get discouraged in the ministry, you ought to go back to the prophecies and other words the Lord spoke to you and use them on the devil!

That's exactly what Paul encouraged Timothy to do when the young man became discouraged. In Second Timothy 1:6, Paul encouraged Timothy to stir up the gifts that were in him, saying, "Wherefore I put thee in remembrance that thou stir up the gift of God, which is in thee by the putting on of my hands."

Then, in First Timothy 1:18, Paul reminded him, "This charge I commit unto thee, son Timothy, according to the prophecies which went before on thee, that thou by them mightest war a good warfare."

Waiting for a Refill

We need to wait on the Lord concerning certain things. Some people, however, don't believe in waiting on God to be refilled. But when that fire of the Holy Spirit in you starts to go out because of hardship and persecution, you have to get a fresh touch from God!

That's what Paul is talking about here — stirring up the gifts, praying in the Holy Spirit, spending time before God, fanning that fire and getting it back to where you can flow again in the things of God. Too many people run out of fuel and never refuel!

Several years ago, I ministered in Germany. There was a heavy anointing in that meeting, and I was preaching along these lines about the anointing of God.

I prayed for a woman who had been full of sickness all her life. The anointing went into her when I laid hands on her. I never had this happen before, but green foam started coming out of her mouth. It was a spirit of sickness and disease that had plagued her.

"Talk About the Anointing"

It was in Germany that God started dealing with me about my anointing. He said, "I want you to talk about the anointing that's in your right hand."

I replied, "But it will look like it's bringing attention to me. Everyone will want me to put my hand on them."

He said, "No, you've got to learn that you must bring attention to *the anointing.*"

As the Bible says, it's the anointing that destroys the yoke, so how can it benefit anyone if they don't know about it?

However, there is a fine line involved where you must not bring attention to yourself. That's the thing that bothered me.

I kept going back and forth on this issue, but the Lord said, "There's nothing wrong with bringing attention to the mantle and the anointing that is on your life."

Many ministers face this dilemma. They don't want to keep telling how the Lord appeared to them. What they need to use to teach their people are the prophecies that went before them.

Do you pastors remember when God spoke to you and told you to go to a certain city? Do you remember the scriptures He gave you? By sharing these scriptures, you're not drawing attention to yourself; you're giving attention to the anointing God told you about.

When Jesus told the people, "The Spirit of the Lord is upon me," that's the way the people found out He was anointed!

There are many different anointings, so drawing on the anointing is not the only way to receive healing. God wants so much for you to be healed that He has put all different types of healing anointings in the Church to meet everyone on their level.

He realizes that not everyone is going to live in the higher realm where you just speak it and believe it, acting on the Word of God. That is the highest way to receive healing.

Chapter 4

The Best Investment I Ever Made

God has a purpose in life for every one of you. You could even be destined to attend a certain meeting. I was, back in 1971, when I attended a Full Gospel Business Men's International meeting in Denver, Colorado.

God had a purpose for my attending this meeting. He told me to attend it. I had to sell my house to take the trip, but it was the best investment I ever made! But you must understand, I sold my house because God instructed me to. Only do something like that at God's direction.

To make a long story short, they were advertising a youth meeting. The speakers included Kenneth E. Hagin, John Osteen and Kenneth Copeland.

I heard Kenneth Copeland and his sermon changed my life. He preached on young David, the covenant man who turned his nation around. I'll never forget it as long as I live. I said, "Man, that's for me!"

I came out of that meeting praising and worshipping God. And out of the corner of my eye I saw a woman lying across two steps that led into another auditorium. This was in the lobby of the Denver Hilton Hotel.

Archie Dennis, the Gospel singer, was standing on the top step praising God. I walked right up to him. I'd never seen anyone fall under the power in my Full Gospel church, so I figured the woman had had a heart attack. I didn't know if they were saying the last rites over her or what.

I asked, "What happened to her?"

Archie said, "Well, she asked me to lay hands on her to get filled with the Holy Ghost, and when I started praying, she started speaking in tongues and fell down under the power of God."

In the meantime, a big crowd of people, pushing and shoving to see better, had gathered around. I was a deacon in a Full Gospel church. I had been saved about six years, and I was in the ministry of helps — cleaning toilets.

A Humbling Experience

I was so hungry for more of God, but I said in my heart, "Lord, I hope You never do that to me in front of all these people!"

BAM! I was slain in the Spirit, too. God may not do something like this to you, but this is my story. People started falling out under the power right in that hotel lobby.

I fell next to the woman who was already on the floor. A *huge* woman who had been standing behind me was the next to fall — and she came down right on top of me! And she stank — oh, the stench! It was awful. God knows how to humble you.

My denomination taught against women preachers, but for some reason or other, I got delivered of prejudice against women preachers down there under that woman. I don't know why; I just did. When I got up, all that prejudice that had been put in me by the church had left me. I'm glad it did.

The Healing Anointing Comes

Paul had his road to Damascus experience, and I had mine. As I lay there, God spoke to me and said, "I'm putting a healing anointing in your right hand."

I didn't know what that was. I didn't know the scripture

22

that says God wrought special miracles by the hands of Paul. No one prophesied this over me; God spoke it to me.

Finally that big woman got up. Then I got up.

She asked, "What happened to you? Something happened to you."

I said, "Yeah," and I kept massaging my right hand. It felt like hot oil was coming out of my hand. It doesn't mean I'm something; it came on me to help the Body of Christ.

She said, "Put your hand on me."

When I did, the power of God went into her body like electricity.

I said, *"My goodness!"*

She was eaten up with cancer. That's why she had such a strong odor. She was so filled with big tumors that her body was enormously bloated, and she had to wear a custom-made dress. When I laid hands on her, it was like a balloon had popped, and her body instantly returned to its normal size.

An 85-year-old man observed this miracle and said, "Hey, young whippersnapper — I've been seeking for the Holy Ghost for 35 years. Lay your hands on *me!*"

When I laid my hands on him, he started speaking in tongues.

I said, *"My goodness!"*

People started falling all over the place. After an hour and a half, people came out into the lobby from the other meetings and found people lying all over the place. I was wringing wet, and my hand still burned.

If I don't tell anyone about this special anointing, how can it benefit the Body of Christ? God showed me it was in the prophet's mantle on my life, and I'm not bringing attention to myself by telling about it. In fact, it's all right to bring attention to the calling or anointing on your life.

We as Word of Faith people need to be careful that we don't back off completely from everything supernatural. We must stay in line with the Word of God on things concerning the anointing in our lives.

"I Ain't No Prophet!"

I guarantee, you'll never operate in the office of a teacher if you don't believe in it and walk in it. When someone prophesied to me years ago that I was going to be a prophet, I said, "You're crazy! The only 'profit' I'm going to make is in business — I'll tell you that right now. I ain't no prophet."

I didn't ask for that anointing. I didn't even know what it was!

After attending the Denver convention, I returned to my home church and began laying hands on the sick. A revival broke out in the youth group in which I was active. People were being healed and stirred up in the church. They got *so* stirred up, I got "the left foot of fellowship" — all because a little boy was healed and got a new hip. They got mad when he was healed! And this all happened in a *Full* Gospel church!

Vanishing Gifts

It's wonderful to see people flow in the gifts of the Spirit. I'm not trying to bring attention to myself when I flow in them; I'm trying to show people the different varieties of gifts you can operate in. If believers don't operate in the gifts, the gifts will disappear from the Church!

If you'll notice, the "generals" of the land always talk about times when God dealt with them and the prophecies they were given. They go back to those times for fresh encouragement to fight the good fight of faith.

Have you ever noticed that the more you talk about the Lord's dealings with someone, the higher the people's faith gets? Pastors know this. They know that when people in their church become discouraged, they've got to retell their vision, or their prophecies, to the people.

When they share these things, they're fighting a good warfare against all the human troublemakers and every spiritual force that's involved. This is what God told us to do through Paul's writings to Timothy.

Never Say Never

Years before, I had made fun of a certain television preacher, and I had bragged, *"I'll* never do what he's doing!" Now I find myself doing some of the very same things! God didn't tell me to say "ba-by" to deaf children, but He did tell me to stick my fingers in their ears and command those deaf spirits to leave them.

Later, I backed off from doing some of those things, but now I'm getting back into some of those different varieties, operations, administrations, and manifestations of the Holy Spirit. We need them all!

In my Fresh Oil Conferences, I try to bring in ministers who have different varieties of anointings so the people can see all the different operations and gifts of the Holy Spirit that God has set in the Church.

Paul said, "For this cause many are weak and sickly among you, and many sleep [die]" (1 Corinthians 11:30). The reason why some churches are weak and sickly spiritually, and many die spiritually, is because the pastors say, "Well, I'll do it all."

You can't do it all, pastor! You need to correctly discern all the different parts that make up the full scope of the Body of Christ.

If you could do it all, it would mean you had the Holy

Spirit in full measure, like Jesus had. But no one has the Spirit in full measure like Jesus.

Send for the Prophet

Many pastors try to do everything, but they can't. If they're having problems in their church, I advise them to get a prophet to come — a true prophet. And when he comes to town, don't tell him all the troubles you've been having.

Let God reveal your problems to him, and let him nail everything. Then your people won't get mad at you, because he'll have "pulled all the stumps out" using spiritual dynamite.

God's Safety Device

We must remember the scriptural admonition that the gifts of the Spirit operate *as the Spirit wills*. I call this a safety device. Just think: If I could control the gifts of healing, I could go around healing everyone, and I could become richer than the doctors.

If the gifts and operations of the Holy Spirit were mine, everyone would look to me. They would say, "Would you come and pray for my loved ones? I'll send a corporate jet for you and give you a million dollars if you'll fly to Australia and pray for my daughter."

People would do exactly that. That's why God has that safety device. That's the reason we don't have "the full measure." We're human beings, and we couldn't handle it. This has been proven in history.

The Man Who Stole the Glory

An English healing evangelist had a special anointing to pray for arthritis. Every person he laid hands on was completely healed of arthritis. Eventually he got puffed up and announced, "I've got the world at my feet."

Several months later, the very thing he had defied came on him. He became so crippled with arthritis he couldn't even move. Why? Because he took the glory. He started bringing attention to himself.

Those with healing anointings must believe healing will happen when they lay their hands on sick people. It won't work unless you *believe* it's going to happen. Notice that Jesus told about His anointing to heal everywhere He went.

The woman with the issue of blood released her faith when she reached Jesus. Why? Because her faith was built up. That's why the people of His day went looking for Him. And that's why the people of our day are *not* looking for our churches. We're not telling them we have an anointing to heal. It's something to think about.

If you really believe what God told you to do in your city, you need to start advertising it, whether it's healing the sick or something else.

God is still anointing people with special anointings. You will see people who are saturated with the anointing of God, but they must remain humble to keep that anointing. And they must stay away from the three G's: gold, glory and girls.

Mere man cannot handle the anointing that was on Jesus. Through the years, the anointing was increased on many, yet they fell because they couldn't handle the glory! I'm referring to being proud and taking the glory due the Lord. Ministers must be so careful of that.

On the other hand, if we keep these things in mind, we shouldn't back off from operating the gifts of the Spirit.

A Different Type of Anointing

Sometimes I operate under a different type of anointing: the prophet's anointing as a seer. God asked Jeremiah, "What *seest* thou?" (Jeremiah 1:11). Jeremiah replied, "I *see* an almond tree."

That was a word of knowledge, yet it goes a little deeper. There's something different when a prophet exercises it; he carries it a bit further. When the prophet finds the person he has *seen*, there's a 100 percent miracle for them every time.

Don't forget: For this cause many are weak and sickly, and many die — because they discern neither the different gifts God has set in the Church nor the variety of operations, administrations, and manifestations of the Holy Spirit.

God set these gifts in the Body for it to profit from them. Sometimes when I would get tired physically, I would start griping, but God would remind me, "I didn't put that anointing on you for you; it's for the people you minister to, so you must continue to go."

Creating an Atmosphere for Miracles

Obedience always creates an atmosphere for miracles. In other words, if you would act on the Word of God, on the inner man when He speaks to you, or when He gives you a vision — just act it out — it will come to pass, as long as it is in line with the Word.

If the devil can keep you in the *past* or in the *future*, he can keep you from your healing. Hebrews 11:1 says, *"Now* faith is the substance of things hoped for."* That means, when hands are laid on you for healing, you're going to receive what *already* belongs to you! You're not going to *get* your healing; you already got it two thousand years ago! It's been provided for you.

Your Point of Contact

Believers make a mistake when they go into a healing line thinking, "When he lays hands on me, I'm going to get my healing." Instead, those in need of healing should confess,

"When hands are laid on me, that is my point of contact that I receive my healing *now,* whether I feel something or not."

Don't say, "I didn't get a hot flash, so I guess I didn't get healed." You got your healing two thousand years ago. The Word of God makes it so clear.

Oh, that we ministers called to the fivefold ministry would wear our mantles with boldness and walk in the anointing and the office that God has called us to walk in; that we would not go in fear and not back up; but we would go with boldness and obey when God speaks to us.

Prophecy

Go back to the time that I spoke to your heart, and then go from there.

I spoke to many to do this and do that, and you didn't do it. Now you've been in disobedience, and it hasn't worked.

Back up to that point. Go back to that prophecy. Go back to when I spoke to you and act on that, and it will all come back together, and you will be in the perfect will of God, saith the Lord of hosts.

Often when we think of being "set free," we think it applies to being set free from devils, but you can be set free from self, or you can be set free from being out of the will of God and be restored back into the will of God.

Some meetings are destined to accomplish this. Unfortunately, many miss out because they say they're "too busy" to attend. In such cases, they miss what God had for them. I sold my house to be at a meeting I was destined to attend. There in Denver God put a portion of the anointing to minister on me.

We please the Lord when we walk humbly before Him and bring attention to the fact that He is the One who is doing the work.

Chapter 5

The Importance of the Anointing

In the past, when people sent me a prayer cloth or a handkerchief, I laid my hands on them and prayed over them when I visited my office.

One day as I was doing this God said, "There's more to this than what you're doing. What you're doing is in accordance with the scripture that says, '...if two of you shall agree on earth as touching any thing...'" (Matthew 18:19).

He added, "If you will notice, Paul *wore* those handkerchiefs. Then, when the anointing came upon him, it went *into* those handkerchiefs. What you're doing is in accordance with agreeing. That's fine, and it will work if the person who gets the handkerchief agrees. But that isn't Acts 19:11. Paul wore them."

You should see me now at my conferences! I tuck prayer cloths all over me and in my pockets and wear them while I minister, and then they are sent to the sick. Why? Because *when the healing anointing comes upon me, it will also go into the cloths.* We've got to get back to the Bible in practices like these.

When prayer cloths are sent to me, I wait until the anointing comes on me, then lay hands on the cloths so the healing anointing can be stored in them and then be transmitted into sick bodies when they are laid on them. That healing anointing isn't on a minister all the time, so I must wait until it's there to transmit it into the cloth.

Out in Left Field With No Anointing

That's why I can't understand some of these so-called prophets who claim they can flow in the prophetic anointing 24 hours a day and give words to people at will.

As I was observing someone minister once, God said, "familiar spirits." People can sound *so* religious. They can even say, "Thus saith the Lord..." But there's a fine line between flesh and spirit, and even prophets can get 'way out in left field' if they're not careful!

They get in trouble when they try to push something that isn't there; when they try to operate in the gifts without the anointing.

And when they do, the devil is quick to step in and accommodate them with words that *sound* like prophecy, but are actually from the soulish realm, or inspired by familiar spirits. It's so sly and slick, you'll even think it's prophecy from God!

False Pastors Abound

Although we're looking at false *prophets,* God told me something once about false *pastors* that shocked me. He said, "There are more false pastors than false prophets in the Body of Christ today."

Think about it: In the natural, people often start a church because there's a need. However, just seeing a need is not the same as fulfilling a call.

You'd better be anointed to start a church. The reason these pastors break down later is because they don't have any "oil," or anointing, in their crankcase!

Many men say they're pastors, but they're just good businessmen. They attend pastors' seminars and may even be good teachers — but that doesn't mean they've been *anointed* to stand in the office of pastor. You must be called to it. It's dangerous to walk in any office if you're not called to it.

This is why a lot of deacons die prematurely: They try to be a pastor and run the church, but they don't have the oil to do it, so they burn out. We've all struggled because of trying to do something God didn't tell us to do, and we didn't have the oil.

Balance in Prayer

I'm also concerned about people who are always fighting devils. All they talk about is devils. They fight devils in the atmosphere and over your city. And they're getting worn out, because they're not fighting under the anointing. Yes, we've got to fight the good fight of faith, but not in the flesh!

What is happening is that intercessors are trying to go into spiritual realms to fight those devils without the necessary equipment or anointing.

You see, *there are certain gifts and equipment necessary for every office.* Why try to tear down a big building with a riding lawn mower? You need a bulldozer to do the job. Likewise, God equips different ministries with the equipment that is necessary to get their job done.

In prayer, the anointing and the necessary spiritual equipment must be on you to deal with certain situations in the spirit realm. God has given you the ability to deal with things that pertain to your own life. But when you get into realms outside of your own life, like trying to pull down spirits over cities, you're laboring in vain if God didn't tell you to do it and equip you with that anointing.

Some intercessors got off a while back, trying to be prophets and prophesy the pastor out of the church, saying he wasn't spiritual, and so forth.

Others kept pushing and pushing as they prayed, and finally they broke into an area of the spirit realm where they had no business being. That's when they got all goofed up. They weren't anointed or equipped to be in that realm!

The Equipment of a True Prophet

I was once privileged, along with some other ministers, to visit with a prophet after a large meeting. We asked questions about the anointing, and he started talking about it.

When you start talking about the anointing, it starts flowing. After this prophet started talking about the anointing, he went into the Spirit for three hours. Long after some people went to bed, he was still sitting there prophesying.

During this time he saw a huge, ugly spirit rising up out of the Atlantic Ocean to attack the United States. This was the real gift of discerning of spirits by one who operates in the prophet's ministry. When he saw it, he promptly dealt with it, because he had the necessary spiritual equipment to go into the spirit realm and deal with it!

"A" for Effort

Everyone who is hungry and tries to accomplish something for God deserves an "A" for effort for trying, but without the oil of anointing, they can't do anything.

You are to come in weakness; not in your strength, but in *God's* strength. For example, you will never touch your city for God without the anointing and without God doing the work. He will do it if you allow Him to.

I've heard of intercessors and others who were trying to do all kinds of weird things in the natural. You've got to be anointed — you've got to have the right equipment — to operate in the spirit realm.

If you attempt to go into outer space in a space ship without wearing the right equipment — a space suit — you won't be able to breathe, and you will probably explode. That's what happens to people who get into the wrong spiritual realm without having the anointing to be there.

Do you remember the sons of Sceva in Acts 19 who tried without any anointing to cast the devil out of someone? The evil spirit in the man beat them up and tore their clothes off! That's what has happened to a lot of the people who are always warring and fighting: The devil beat them up! Look at their faces — they're drawn with fatigue, because they're worn out.

Talk About Jesus

In addition, the devil is operating in their home. Bad things are happening to them. Why? Because warring is all they talk about, the devil accommodates them and launches war on them. *I talk about Jesus!*

When you go around saying you're a prophet, if you aren't careful, you'll force yourself out into the spirit realm, and the devil will accommodate you. He'll ambush you! You'll get hurt if you don't have the oil, the equipment, and the anointing to deal with him when you're outside of your area of authority.

Yes, there are true prophets, but you must be anointed to stand in this office. There is a great deal of persecution connected with the office, so don't try to be a prophet without having the prophet's anointing! You'll be persecuted enough just preaching the Word.

Jesus got up before the people in Nazareth and declared, "God has anointed Me." What was their reaction? They tried to push Him off a cliff — because of the anointing. The devil doesn't want you to flow in the anointing, either, because it's the anointing that destroys his work!

The Devil Fights the Anointing

Can you see how the devil has slipped into the Church, trying to abort what God wants to do in the Spirit through these different varieties of ministries? The devil is trying to get us to do things in the flesh. He's trying to abort the ministry of the prophets, the apostles, and every other office and gift.

Have you noticed the lyrics of contemporary worship songs? They declare, *"We're* going to do this. *We're* going to take this. *We're* going to do this."* There's nothing in the songs about the blood of Jesus or what Jesus did at Calvary. We must always remember that we are victorious only because of what Jesus did.

The Anointing Visits Strategic Meetings

We may be missing God by having short meetings. It takes about a week just to break through all the junk anyway. Then people get on the phone and tell their friends, "Something is happening over here." That's just the way human beings are.

In the future, we will see meetings continue for several weeks. Miracles will happen, revival will break out, and the revival will keep on growing.

A pastor told me he invited a popular speaker to his church, and the place was jammed. But the next day, when they went out to clean the parking lot, they found it full of beer cans and cigarette butts. Why? A lot of those people came just for the miracles. But at least they were coming to church!

I have learned that God has *strategic* meetings when He wants to impart something in the Spirit to mature believers. He keeps carnal people away from these meetings when He wants to do something special.

Follow the Cloud

The gifts of the Holy Spirit are important. The Word is important. We need them all, because the Word is life. If something isn't in the Word, I don't want it, because I am determined to follow God's Word and the leading of the Holy Spirit.

God gave us spiritual gifts and His Word so we will be strong. We will receive a blessing from discerning the Lord's Body and from studying the twelfth and thirteenth chapters of

First Corinthians, learning how the gifts of the Spirit and the love of God affect the Body of Christ.

Whoever follows the Word of God will go with the "cloud" of God's presence. If you go with the "cloud," it had better be in line with the Word of God!

There are lots of "clouds" out there, but few of them have any rain in them. I want to go with a cloud that has rain in it — a cloud that will produce — a cloud that has the power, the lightning, and the thunder of God in it!

Chapter 6

The Anointing and the New Revival

In the last few years, we have been in the babyhood stages of a great revival. Soon we will step through the door of the supernatural into the full revival God wants for these last days.

Then we will see the fivefold ministry develop as the Head of the Church wills, and we will walk in it. The coming revival may not come the way we think it should; nevertheless, however it comes, it will be powerful.

There will be men and women who will walk in awesome power in this new revival — but the ministers you were certain would be used as leaders will not go with the revival.

Those whom God will use in this revival will recognize that they came from nowhere and from nothing. They will humble themselves before God and say, "Lord, not my will, but thine be done. I don't care to be seen by anyone. I just want what You want. Use that other person instead of me."

I've met people like this. They have a stronger anointing than others, and they will do exploits, because *in the new revival we will experience a dimension of the Spirit that the Church hasn't seen yet.*

Unless we have a genuine revival soon, a whole generation of ministers will arise who will not recognize the movings of the Holy Spirit or how to flow in the things of the Spirit.

Make Room for the Holy Spirit

One of the reasons for this is, we've gotten into a rut in

most of our church services. We sing a certain number of songs, preach for 30 to 45 minutes, and then we all go home!

The Holy Spirit likes to come in and speak, but ministers don't understand this, so they don't give Him that opportunity. They go on with their program and cut everything else out.

The reason why witchcraft has permeated even into the Church is because *our children haven't seen the supernatural.* That's why, when I feel in my spirit that we are going to be in a powerful meeting, I want my son right on the front row so he can be around the anointing. I want him to be familiar with God's presence.

So let it be said that we are *not* going to lose a generation of ministers who do not know how to operate in the Spirit; but this will be a generation that will know the movings and the flow of the Spirit, and they will flow with power and equipment from on high, with the Word of God in their mouths.

Let it be said that this generation of ministers will have anointing and ability from heaven to accomplish those things God has called them to do; and much rejoicing and much harvest will come because of the obedience of God's servants.

Now I want to share some spiritual advice and some practical advice to help this new generation of young ministers mature in the things of God.

Pitfalls for Young Preachers

Just because you've got the gifts operating through you doesn't mean you're someone special. All of us should have the gifts of the Holy Spirit flowing in our lives.

I wonder how many ministries have been destroyed when men tried to promote them with the flesh instead of allowing God to promote them.

Some people use the route of politicking — getting close to the right people and flattering them — to get to the top. Watch out when people tell you how great and wonderful you are, because they're puffing you up for something they want from you!

My wife protects me from that. After we get in the car after a meeting, she says, "Don't you believe that woman who just told you what a great preacher you are. You are special to me, but you stay humble before God."

Nancy and I often discuss how famous men and women of God in past generations were destroyed through pride, and how we can learn from their examples.

Paul on Preaching

One of the most important things ministers must build into their life is *character*. Let's look at Paul's advice to Timothy about the ministry:

> **This is a true saying, If a man desire the office of a bishop, he desireth a good work.**
>
> **A bishop then must be blameless, the husband of one wife, vigilant, sober, of good behaviour, given to hospitality, apt to teach;**
>
> **Not given to wine, no striker, not greedy of filthy lucre; but patient, not a brawler, not covetous;**
>
> **One that ruleth well his own house, having his children in subjection with all gravity....**
>
> *Not a novice, lest being lifted up with pride he fall into the condemnation of the devil.*
>
> **1 Timothy 3:1-4,6**

"Novice" means a baby Christian or a young believer. Some pastors have had the unhappy experience of taking a novice under their wing and training him for a number of years until one day he got mad about something, split the church, went down the street, and started another church.

That's unethical. You shouldn't do such a thing. God sees it, it hurts the Body of Christ, and it will hurt your ministry.

The Sad Story of a Novice

I know of a young man who had the gifts of healing operating through him in a mighty way. In fact, great miracles occurred in his meetings.

Although this young man was still a novice, and he hadn't proven himself yet, a television station started to promote his ministry. They built him up so much on TV that large crowds started coming to hear him.

Three years ago, this young man died of AIDS. He had ended up working as a waiter in a Hollywood restaurant before his death.

Once he'd had a powerful ministry in the Spirit, but men promoted a novice in the flesh, which is a very dangerous thing to do. He got lifted up with pride, and it destroyed his life and ministry.

Starting at the Bottom

When you start in the ministry, you will start at the bottom and sometimes make great sacrifices, but the call alone will pull you through if you remain faithful to it.

Of course, most people want to start at the top! I've seen many who pushed themselves to get to the top, but they're not around anymore. They went right back down again.

If you think you are called to a particular office, just wait and test it to find out for sure. Even if you *are* called to it, you won't step into it immediately. I didn't step into the prophet's ministry immediately; I started in the ministry of helps.

Too many people say, "Well, bless God, I'm a prophet," and they want to get up on the platform and begin to operate in that office right away. They don't realize there are things they must do and learn first.

If God fully exposed them to that office too soon, they

would destroy themselves, their ministries, their families, and others.

Preparation time is not lost time. I have celebrated my twenty-eighth anniversary in the ministry, and although I learned many valuable lessons during those years, I feel like I know very little. In fact, I feel like I'm just getting started!

The Spirit of Competition

I learned about novices the hard way. Once I put a novice in a position he wasn't ready for. He was all excited about it, but I gave him too much responsibility, and he got prideful and turned on me.

As Paul pointed out, pride is a problem with novices. You've got to watch out for it. And pride is often accompanied by a spirit of competition.

The spirit of competition you sometimes see among Christians isn't the Spirit of God at all; it's the spirit of the world in manifestation.

Be sweet, and be a gentleman or a lady in your business dealings and in all the other aspects of your life. After all, we are not supposed to be in the world, behaving as the unsaved do, stepping on each other to get to the top and fulfill our own ambitions!

Little Pastor or Big Apostle?

Once I preached in a church pastored by a novice. The power of God came on me, and I fell out under God's power. I then rose up and prophesied and ministered to the people.

After I left, the pastor told a friend of mine, "You know, Ed Dufresne couldn't take it at our church, because the anointing in my pulpit was too strong for him!" That's ridiculous! We're not in competition.

This young man had started his church in an area of the

country that was enjoying phenomenal growth. He had only been saved for six years, and because he became successful in a short time, he thought he was something special. And because he was a novice, pride entered his heart.

Then some fellow came to town and prophesied that the young pastor was an apostle over that city, so he started going around telling everyone that he was the apostle of that city because he had a church of 2,000 members.

But just because you've got a church of 2,000 doesn't mean you're a big shot. You ought to thank God, submit to some men who have been around a while, and use some wisdom about things.

As we were leaving that city, not knowing what the pastor had said about me, I told the man who traveled with me, "Watch what happens. Within two years that pastor will have fewer than 250 people." Within two years, he lost most of those people, and his attendance went down to 220. His problems were caused by pride.

Now I understand he's starting to get turned around a little. He could have avoided that episode altogether if he had only taken some advice I gave him while I was there. But he wouldn't listen.

The people from his church scattered all over. Some time later, when I held a meeting in that city, the auditorium was filled with many beat-up sheep that were hurt because their pastor wanted to operate outside his calling.

Be careful that men don't exalt you above your character, because it takes time to build character.

The Man Who Would Be Pastor

I pastored for 11 1/2 years, and you learn some things in that length of time. A young man came up to me once and said, "You know, I could pastor this church better than you're pastoring it. I'm a lot smarter than you, and I went to such-and-such school."

I said, "Big deal!" I wasn't angry; it was just the Holy Spirit within me. I asked him, "How many churches have you pastored?"

"I haven't pastored any."

"Well, go out and pastor a few. When you get some experience, maybe I'll take some of your advice. In the meantime, instruct yourself. God set *me* as the pastor of this church, and I'm the one He anointed for it."

He went off and said I didn't have any *love*. That's the usual excuse Charismatics give when they're corrected!

Do not offer novices position and authority while they are still immature. Let them prove themselves. If they believe they have something, do them a favor and let them serve in lesser capacities first.

Stay in Your Office

Be sure you walk and remain in the office to which God has called you. Intruding into the wrong office can kill you! Remember, in Old Testament times when anyone who was not anointed to be High Priest intruded into the Holy of Holies, he dropped dead.

We're under grace today, and it takes a little longer to die. I'm convinced, however, that many pastors have heart attacks, ulcers, and other health problems because *they're doing things they were not called and anointed to do.*

I'm thinking of a man who is a strong businessman. He's really called to the ministry of helps, but he wants to be a pastor. There are people all over the country who are like him: They aren't called to it, but they want to pastor.

If this businessman doesn't recognize his error, he won't

live out his full lifetime. Why? Because he's *intruding* into that office. He isn't called to it; he isn't equipped for it; and he doesn't have the anointing to serve in it.

A Danger in the Fivefold Ministry

So when you try to walk in something you're not called to, it can cause you to die prematurely. Many people don't realize this about the fivefold ministry.

They think, "Well, bless God, I can do anything I want to. I can walk in any office I want to." No, you *can't* walk in any office you want to — not unless God calls you into that office and anoints and equips you for it.

People who try to walk in the prophet's ministry without the anointing may pick up familiar spirits. You may know in your heart that someday you'll operate in the office of a prophet, but you still need to take time to develop.

"Yes, but Jesus is coming next year! What am I going to do?" Just relax in your gift. Just relax in the Holy Spirit.

These practical things I'm sharing with you will help get you into the spirit realm. They will enable you to walk in the anointing God has given you.

How to Lose Your Effectiveness

There's another danger in trying to walk in an office that isn't yours: You will lose your effectiveness for God. For example, if a pastor tries to step out and be an apostle when he isn't called to be an apostle, he will fail.

Be careful about this. You can have a big, growing church and all of a sudden decide, "Well, we ought to have our own ministerial group, and we ought to have this, and we ought to do that." (Actually, seasoned ministers and ministries should be handling such things.)

I know of a church whose pastor said, "We're big. We're

strong. We've got a lot of money." He started doing things God never called him to do.

Like anyone else, I have made the same mistake: I got out of my anointing. I am not an administrator, but I tried to administrate in the natural. I messed everything up because I got out of my anointing, so I hired someone with the anointing to do the work of an administrator.

I don't want to put fear in you so you won't operate in the gifts of the Spirit. I just want to teach you some things so you can tell the difference between a familiar spirit and the Spirit of God, and between the works of the flesh and the works of the Holy Spirit so you will flow stronger in your God-given gift.

More practical advice that will help you get into the spirit realm is: Don't be taken up with names or titles. Humble yourself under the mighty hand of God, and let Him promote you.

Also, realize that you cannot build your ministry on the supernatural or the gifts. To survive, it must be built on the Word of God.

If you get off into things God hasn't called you to do, you will not only lose the effectiveness of your anointing; you will wear yourself out, because you don't have the oil, or anointing, to do those things. Then your spiritual bearings will burn out!

Veering Off Into Big Projects

By doing things you are not called to do, a minister can easily get off into error. One of the best examples of this was John Alexander Dowie.

Dowie was one of the first in his century to have a mighty healing ministry, but then he decided to build the city of Zion, Illinois, for his followers. (You can read his thought-provoking story in Gordon Lindsay's biography, *John Alexander Dowie,* published by Christ For the Nations.)

Ministers must check their motives before they start big projects. They must make sure that whatever they are doing is because God told them to do it, and it will glorify God, not man. (Then He will supply the money for it.)

This information will keep you from making the same mistakes other men and women have made. It will keep you on the right track. Then you can say, "I am making a note of that. I am not going to veer off course. I will stay true. I will stay firm. I choose to do *only* the things God told me to do."

Chapter 7

Degrees and Rankings of Anointings

> I beseech you therefore, brethren, by the mercies of God, that ye present your bodies a living sacrifice, holy, acceptable unto God, which is your reasonable service.
>
> And be not conformed to this world: but be ye transformed by the renewing of your mind, that ye may prove what is that good, and acceptable, and perfect, will of God.
>
> Romans 12:1,2

If you want to walk in the perfect will of God for your life, the Bible says there are two things you need to work on: (1) your body, and (2) your mind. Both are in the way!

This means that I must first present my body as "a living sacrifice." Because a sacrifice *dies,* my body must die to human desires in order to fulfill God's desires. So, once I am dead to what *I* want, God can use me as *He* wants.

Other characteristics of dying to self include these:
Dead men do not strike back.
Dead men do not gossip.
Dead men do not gripe, "I've got to travel all over, stay in hotel rooms, and do thus and so."

The second thing you must do to walk in the perfect will of God is to renew that squirrely mind of yours in the area of your calling. In fact, you must renew it in *every* area of life, "...that ye may prove what is that good, and acceptable, and perfect, will of God" (Romans 12:2).

I don't know about you, but my goal is to walk in the

49

perfect will of God for my life!

The Measure of Faith

For I say, through the grace given unto me, to every man that is among you, not to think of himself more highly than he ought to think; but to think soberly, according as God hath dealt to every man the measure of faith.

Romans 12:3

Everyone has the measure of faith — I believe that. But I also believe, after further study in this passage, that God is referring here to *the measure of faith for ministry.*

I believe that when God equips you for the ministry, He gives you the measure of faith necessary to believe for what you need to get your job done.

There are different degrees and rankings of all the offices in the fivefold ministry. Every ministry gift carries ranks within that office.

Gifts Differing

As the sixth verse says:

Having then gifts differing according to the grace that is given to us, **whether prophecy, let us prophesy according to** *the proportion of faith.*

Romans 12:6

No matter what your ranking is, you are rewarded according to your faithfulness in that rank.

I've heard people say, "I'm going over to Joe's church to see what they're doing. If I do what they're doing, I'll be successful, too."

These people are missing the whole point: Get before God and find the plan He has for *you.* Then God will honor what He told *you* to do. That will eliminate the competition and jealousy that are rampant today among Christians.

I visit churches, admire their beautiful buildings and millions of dollars' worth of television equipment, and sometimes am tempted to wonder, "Why don't I have all these things?" The reason is, I don't *need* all those things for the ranking I have.

Yield to Others' Abilities

We must recognize each other's abilities, or gifts, and yield to them when necessary.

My wife is an evangelist. I'm going to help her more in her tent meetings, but mostly, as a prophet, I speak to the Body of Christ, not to the unsaved. Nancy and I flow together and help one another in ministry. When she's in my meetings and has something from the Spirit, I yield to her anointing.

For example, because she's an evangelist, I let her have the altar calls. Because of her anointing in that area, she gets more people saved than I do. I'm not a front man; I'm a "stump puller" in the Spirit.

Not long ago, I went to a very large church. For two weeks before I got there, the pastors had taught about "the different guy who is coming." Everyone introduced me as "a different guy." I thought, "What's wrong with me?" Then I got offended over it! It was just my pride, because I wanted to be known as "the dignified teacher Ed Dufresne." (With my background, not having much of an education, sometimes pride can step in.)

I went back to my hotel room and complained, "Lord, I don't care for that kind of an introduction, thank You. They say I'm *different*. I wonder what everyone is saying about me? I've had enough persecution elsewhere without them saying I'm different, too!"

"I'm Different"

Then God gave me a sermon. The next day I preached it. It

was entitled, "I'm Different!" First Corinthians 12:5-7 says that there are differences of administrations, diversities of operations, and different manifestations.

I told those people, "I'm scriptural: I'm different!" Hallelujah, there isn't another person like me on the face of this earth!

If I were still the old sinner Ed Dufresne, I would be engaged in fist fights at times. Fortunately, that old Ed Dufresne is dead. I'm a new creature in Christ. Otherwise, to tell you the truth, I'd probably be in jail.

My Boat Can't Sink!

Human beings are very interesting. Their adulation can quickly turn to forgetfulness. When you're popular and well-known, people can cause you to burn out with overwork if you don't pace yourself.

You can be a famous minister, die, and within six months your church will have another pastor. Eventually, they will forget about you. They won't even put flowers on your grave!

I've been in situations where I thought I was sinking. It looked like my whole ministry was going under, and I was going to drown. Most of your so-called friends forsake you when it looks like your ship is sinking.

One day I said, "God, I'm sinking; I'm sinking!"

God replied, "How can you sink when you've got Jesus in your boat?"

You must understand, God won't test you with evil, but He will *prove* you to see if you have faith.

Many times my back has been against the wall. Some of my staff left me. They said, "This boat is sinking. I'm jumping out!"

Do you know what the Lord told me about this? He said,

"When the water comes up, it's an opportunity to get rid of all the rats."

I'm Still Floating

My boat bobbed back up. I'm still floating, and I'm not planning on sinking. I'm not going to be shipwrecked, because I'm not a "shooting star" that appears on the scene for a brief season. I'm in this for the long haul. When all the dust settles, I'm still going to be here! I've made my decision: I'm still going to be around!

That's why I haven't built my ministry on the gifts of the Spirit or the gift of the prophet. I have built it on the Word of God. I always start with the Word, and if the Spirit wants to move, fine.

Faith for Your Task

God never gives a minister a bigger job than His gift of faith. When God speaks to you and tells you to do something, *He will give you the measure of faith necessary to get that job done.*

If He tells you to go on national television, He'll pay the bills. You won't need gimmicks.

This comes right back to the question of motive: *What is your motive?* You may do all right for a while, but if your motive isn't right, if your heart isn't right, you'll destroy yourself.

God isn't putting up with any more gimmicks! All that Hollywood junk is coming out of the Body of Christ. It won't work to have man exalt you if you don't have the goods! I'd rather have God exalt me. Then my promotion will last, because it will be built on a solid foundation.

Two Kinds of Faith

It's important to realize that the faith, or grace, God

gives us to accomplish our *calling* has nothing to do with our *personal faith*. Romans 12:3 says, "Through the grace given unto me...." This means, through the *ability* that God has given me, I am doing these things.

Paul was a man just like you and me, but grace was given to him to fulfill his calling. Get into the will of God and find out what your *grace* is.

If you don't know what you're called to do, simply walk in the *ability* you have right now. If you're a carpenter, be a carpenter. If you're a police officer, be a police officer.

The Importance of Obedience

The Holy Spirit has different ways of doing things, but *obedience always creates an atmosphere for the demonstration of God's power in miracles.*

We were taught in the Word of Faith Movement that we could have *whatever* we said. However, we've got to understand this promise in context. Making a faith confession is like using a pen. Speaking the confession writes on your heart, and you believe what you're saying. However, you can't confess something that's beyond your grace in the ministry.

"I'm going to have a TV ministry. I'm going to have a TV ministry. I'm going to have a TV ministry."

Yes, that's your confession, but did God *call* you to have a TV ministry?

"Why, He said to go into all the world and preach the Gospel!"

That's stretching it. People use that excuse for everything. They'll visit a church and decide they want the same kind of sophisticated television equipment God allowed that church to have and be stewards over. What happens is, that person is believing for the equipment out of his own lust.

"Well, I want that. I want to get in front of everyone. I

want to be a minister. I want..." *You* want. No, it's what *God* wants.

Spiritual Responsibility

The things I'm sharing with you in this book can save your ministry and your life. I know what I'm talking about, because I did a lot of stupid things as I was growing up spiritually. My heart was right, but my thinking wasn't always right!

That's what Paul was talking about: He told us to renew our minds. He also warned us not to think of ourselves more highly than we ought. Just because we have more ability and grace to reach more people than the pastor of a 250 member church doesn't mean we're greater than he is. In fact, with our grace comes greater responsibility.

William Branham was a tremendous man of God. But he made up his mind he was going to be a teacher, even though he was called to be a prophet. Since he was out of his calling, he began teaching false doctrine.

God couldn't allow that, because it would harm the whole body of Christ, and Brother Branham was removed off the scene. The devil had an open door to destroy him, and he did.

Brother Branham is in heaven with the Lord now, but if he hadn't gotten out of his grace and into error, do you realize he would still be ministering?

He could have ministered during the sixties, the seventies, the eighties, even until the present day, and we would have learned from that powerful gift he had of the word of knowledge and the word of wisdom.

Ministry Ranking

You see, *when high-ranking ministers fail in some way, all those under them are automatically affected!* The greater your rank within your office, the more people you will affect.

Ministry ranking is parallel to *military* ranking. In other words, Satan's ranking is parallel to God's ranking. So when God's general knocks out Satan's general, it automatically affects the devils in lower ranks.

God's generals deal with Satan's generals, lieutenants deal with lieutenants, corporals with corporals, captains with captains, and so forth.

It's good to have prophets come to your church, because of the spiritual equipment they've got. You need to recognize each office in the fivefold ministry. A teacher will come to your church and deposit certain things. So will an apostle and a prophet, according to their gifts.

In some cases, if you stand in more than one office, you can go back and forth between the anointings. For example, I weave in and out between the prophet's office and the teacher's office.

As you grow and mature in the things of God, usually one office will start to be stronger than the others, and you will walk in that higher rank. More responsibilities come with the higher rank.

The Temptation to "Perform"

If you're not careful, you can push someone to "perform," and once they start, it will create a demand for them to continue to perform. Unfortunately, that's what's happening with prophets today. *But ministers are not called to perform!*

"Ed was with Pastor So-and-so and this and that happened. Ed was over there and raised $100,000 in five minutes. BAM! — he got it. I'll get him over to my church to do that."

I don't want to hurt anyone — because I believe there are true moves of God in what is happening — but it's wrong to advertise, "Come to our meeting. We're going to give everyone a word." That's a bunch of baloney. It's *as the Spirit wills.*

If you minister in the gifts, don't feel obligated to *perform.*

If the Spirit doesn't manifest, don't you try to do something in the flesh. If you try to perform or force something to happen, you will open yourself up to listen to a familiar spirit, because you will be off the Word of God.

A prophet's ministry cannot be built on the supernatural; it must be built on the Word. The prophet should operate in the spiritual gifts, but he must build his ministry on the preaching and the teaching gift.

If you keep the flow in the spiritual gifts secondary, it will guard you from being sucked in by familiar spirits. Ministering the Word must be your primary objective.

How to Recognize Familiar Spirits

There can be a fine line between a familiar spirit and the Holy Spirit.

Familiar spirits always attract attention to a person and uplift that person instead of Jesus.

This, then, is the test: If it brings attention to the man or the woman who is ministering instead of causing worship of Jesus, it's the work of a familiar spirit.

When the gifts are in operation, people may start to worship the minister. They say, "Oh, isn't he something!" You must beware of that kind of display, because it's another spiritual snare.

That's why I often walk out of a meeting after I'm done. That way God gets all the praise and glory. After all, He did it; we didn't!

Other Spirits

A so-called preacher who got into error told a man, "You own a valuable ring. You lost it, and I'll tell you where it is: It's in the lower drawer where you keep your clothing. It's underneath, over in the corner. You're supposed to bring that ring and give it to me for the ministry."

This happened because a familiar spirit knew where the ring was, and he told the preacher. The fallen preacher then took the ring, sold it, and kept the money for himself. He said he knew the location of the ring through God's gift. No, it was through the familiar spirit.

Realize there are other spirits out there in the spiritual realm. That's why you must be properly equipped spiritually, and you must have accurate spiritual discernment.

Some of you want to operate under a heavy anointing, like an experienced prophet does, but you hardly know how to get in out of the rain yet, to say nothing of recognizing those anointings. Don't get mad at me; this is meant to help you.

God gave the ministering gifts for what? For the perfecting of the saints, for the work of the ministry, and for the edifying of the Body. Therefore, all ministering gifts must recognize each other's role in the Body and operate in unity.

For example, the prophet is to inspire the teacher. The teacher is then to study what God says through the prophet and teach the Body in clarity and balance what God is saying. How beautifully this unity brings growth and maturity to God's people.

We ought to listen to what the true prophets of the land are saying.

Chapter 8

Oiled by the Anointing

I therefore, the prisoner of the Lord, beseech you that ye walk worthy of the vocation [calling] wherewith ye are called.

Ephesians 4:1

How many of you know you're called? Before I was saved, I certainly had no idea there was a calling on my life. I knew I loved God, however.

I used to sit in bars and get in fights with people who would say there is no God. I'd hit them over the head with a beer bottle and say, "Yes, there *is* a God!" (Like He needed me to fight for Him).

One night I was sitting on a bar stool, minding my own business — I wasn't bothering God, and I wasn't bothering the devil; I was drunk — and a voice came to me and said, "You're going to preach. You're going to go all over the world preaching My Gospel."

I told the bartender, "Joe, set everyone up with a beer. I'm going to be *a priest!*" And they all laughed and drank my beer. I was raised as a Catholic, so I thought I was going to be a priest.

A month later, I went to a Protestant church with a man who had been witnessing to me. I got saved in that church in 1965, and immediately wanted to serve the Lord.

I started in the ministry of helps, because I couldn't get up in front of people and speak. I couldn't even give my testimony in church.

However, God knows people's hearts, and He will use anyone. Once He used a jackass to prophesy to a disobedient prophet, and that should keep our pride level down!

I just don't understand people like that prophet — people who have tasted the good things of God and say, "Well, my spouse left me, so I'm quitting the ministry."

What does *that* have to do with your relationship with God? Are you going to go to hell for a woman? Are you going to go to hell for a man?

I don't understand people who complain, "I went into the ministry, and it got kind of rough." What did you think would happen? Did you think the devil was going to roll over, play dead, and allow you to invade his territory? You will have some rough times in the ministry!

My First Speaking Engagement

There was that call on my life, and I couldn't get away from it. I'll never forget the first time I had an invitation to preach. My church invited me to speak to the youth.

I got turned on to the Word of God by Kenneth Copeland tapes — the big, five-inch reels that we had then — so I took a big tape recorder to the youth meeting, set the machine on the pulpit, and announced, "All right, I can't preach — but here's Ken Copeland."

Then I pushed the PLAY button, sat down, and listened while Brother Copeland preached to the youth for a whole hour. I thought I couldn't preach, but I knew I *could* believe for miracles, so I prayed for the sick afterwards. We had all kinds of miracles and healings.

This is the way I "preached" from then on, lugging my heavy tape recorder around and depending on Ken Copeland for the taped messages.

God Takes My Crutch Away

Then one day God told me to leave that tape recorder home. It scared me! "My Lord," I pleaded, *"wait a minute!* I'm not going to get up in front of people and make a fool of myself! I'm not a public speaker; never have been. *I'm not going to do it!"*

Once you've got a call on your life, its tug is inescapable. God has ways of making it inescapable, too! After God dealt firmly with me, I finally said, "Well, maybe I could get up and give a *little* testimony..."

Later God said to me, "I have anointed your lips; man hasn't. Open your mouth, and I will fill it. Study to show yourself approved, and I will fill your mouth."

I admire preachers who can get up and preach a whole sermon off just one word they've heard. That's a gift from God. Man can't put that in you, but God can put it in you. Glory to God, He has put it in me!

The First Time I Preached

I'll never forget the first time I got up and really preached. I opened my mouth, and after half an hour, I said to myself, "My Lord, I didn't know I knew that!"

Praise God for the vocation, the calling, that's on our lives.

Let's read further in Ephesians 4:

> **With all lowliness and meekness, with longsuffering, forbearing one another in love.**
>
> **Ephesians 4:2**

A lot of people don't know anything about longsuffering and forbearing (which means to put up with each other when we don't agree with each other). I've been tested on that one!

For example, some people always want to know, "What

camp are you in? We don't know where you're *at.*"

A Spirit of Division

I know right away that they're trying to "locate" me to see if they're going to fellowship with me or not. But that's a spirit of division. It's not of God, and I don't want anything to do with it.

I don't go around worrying, "I wonder what So-and-so thinks about that?" The important thing is: *What does God say about it?* We're afraid of man when we ought to be more afraid of God and what He says in His Word.

However, I attempt to reply to those questions with longsuffering, forbearance, and love. I say, "Well, brother, right now I'm not in any camp. I'm just following God's Spirit, and I'm watching the Head of the Church, who is Jesus."

You may be doctrinally correct in some areas, but your attitude can stink, you can be out of love, and your church can be dead. There are a lot of folks down in the graveyard who are real dignified, too.

Beware of Wet Blankets

When you've got God in you and all over you, something's bound to happen!

When I first got saved, I attended a Full Gospel church, but after I got turned on to the Word of God, they yelled, "Wild fire, wild fire, wild fire!"

They tried to put my fire out. Their "wet blankets" were soaked with unbelieving water. They tried to throw this unbelief water on me to extinguish my faith fire.

They told me, "Now, you just be *sweet,* Ed. You used to be a sweet usher, but now you're *wild!* You're praying for people, and tumors are disappearing and a youngster's hips were put back in place."

Prosperity and Dignity

They got all upset — and this was supposed to be a *Full* Gospel church. What happened to that church is happening today in thousands of churches. They get prosperous, move to the "right" side of the tracks, and get dignified.

"Now we're respected," they say, and they grab their wet blankets anytime there's a little fire. I'd rather put up with a little wildfire than have no fire at all!

> **With all lowliness and meekness, with longsuffering, forbearing one another in love;**
>
> **Endeavouring to keep the unity of the Spirit in the bond of peace.**
>
> **There is one body, and one Spirit, even as ye are called in one hope of your calling;**
>
> **One Lord, one faith, one baptism,**
>
> **One God and Father of all, who is above all, and through all, and in you all.**
>
> **But unto every one of us is given grace according to the measure of the gift of Christ.**
>
> **Ephesians 4:2-7**

This last statement is where a lot of people miss it. They fail to find out what the grace, or calling, on their life is and what they are supposed to do with that calling. If they don't do what God has called them to do, they could face many problems.

Burning the Bearings Out

Ministers can lose their effectiveness in what God called them to do when they get involved in other things. People pull them into other things, and before they know it, they're not as effective in ministry as they once were.

You can become involved in good things that will rob you of your anointing and even lead to your premature death, as we saw in a previous chapter.

Ministers plunge into all kinds of activities, but they're not always successful, no matter how hard they try. This prompted me to ask God about it.

He said, "They're doing things that I didn't give them the oil to do, so their bearings burn out."

When you see a successful church, you must not get jealous and decide, "Well, I think I'll start a church here, too." You can't simply copy that successful pastor. You need an anointing to start a church.

God gave that successful pastor the oil to do it, but it doesn't mean He'll give you the oil to start a church in the same town. It may not be His will for you.

You must be led by the Holy Spirit for God to use you in your grace. Then He will give you the oil you need for *your* job.

God Rewards Faithfulness

God gives different abilities and equipment to get different jobs done. He will reward you according to the grace He gave you. For example, He would be unfair if He judged pastors simply by numbers.

A man with a small church on the outskirts of a city may have pastored there all his life, but if he was faithful to that small flock and to the will of God, he is deemed faithful in the eyes of God, and he will get the same reward as the equally faithful pastor of a large flock.

Pinch yourself and say, "I'm just flesh." Unless you've got the oil and the anointing — unless God gives you the ability — you aren't going to make it in the ministry.

"Charisma" alone isn't going to do it! To be successful, your ministry must be oiled by the anointing of the Holy Spirit.

God's Gifts to Men

Wherefore he saith, When he ascended up

on high, he led captivity captive, and gave
gifts unto men.

(Now that he ascended, what is it but that he
also descended first into the lower parts of
the earth?

He that descended is the same also that
ascended up far above all heavens, that he
might fill all things.)

Ephesians 4:8-10

Jesus ascended into heaven "and gave gifts unto men." What
were some of those gifts? We referred to them previously in
Chapter 1. Let's look at the next verse: "And he gave some,
apostles; and some, prophets; and some, evangelists; and some,
pastors and teachers" (Ephesians 4:11).

First Corinthians 12:18 says that God "set" certain gifts in
the Church: "But now hath God set the members every one of
them in the body, as it hath pleased him."

It's very important when God "sets," or establishes, a work.
Are you familiar with the properties of concrete? You can move
it or do anything you want with it as long as it's wet. But once
it sets up, you can't move it.

When God sets you in the church, your calling is firm.

Books by Ed Dufresne

Anointings & Mantles

Fresh Oil From Heaven

Praying God's Word

Faithfulness: The Key To Divine Promotion

Devil Don't Touch My Stuff

There's a Healer in the House

The Prophet: Friend of God

For a complete list of tapes and books by Ed Dufresne, to be on his mailing list, and to receive his quarterly newsletter, *Jesus the Healer*, please write:

Ed Dufresne Ministries
P.O. Box 186
Temecula, CA 92593